World Book's Documenting History
The Chinese Revolution

中國人民解放軍東北野戰軍
政治部宣傳隊

毛主席

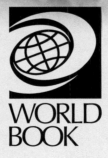

WORLD
BOOK

a Scott Fetzer company
Chicago

www.worldbookonline.com

World Book, Inc.
233 N. Michigan Avenue
Chicago, IL 60601
U.S.A.

For information about other World Book publications, visit our Web site at **http://www.worldbookonline.com**
or call **1-800-WORLDBK (967-5325)**.

For information about sales to schools and libraries, call **1-800-975-3250 (United States)**, or **1-800-837-5365 (Canada)**.

Library of Congress Cataloging-in-Publication Data

The Chinese Revolution.
  p. cm. -- (World Book's documenting history)
  Summary: "A history of the Communist revolution in China, based on primary source documents and other historical artifacts. Features include period art works and photographs; excerpts from literary works, letters, speeches, broadcasts, and diaries; summary boxes; a timeline; maps; and a list of additional resources"-- Provided by publisher.
  Includes bibliographical references and index.
  ISBN 978-0-7166-1503-3   8497
  1. China--History--20th century--Juvenile literature. 2. China--History--20th century--Sources--Juvenile literature. 3. Revolutions --China--History--20th century--Juvenile literature. 4. Revolutions --China--History--20th century--Sources--Juvenile literature.
I. World Book, Inc.
DS774.C4425 2011
951.05--dc22
                                              2010020354

World Book's Documenting History
Set ISBN 978-0-7166-1498-2
Printed in Malaysia by TWP Sdn Bhd, JohorBahru
1st printing September 2010

Contents

Winds of Change

CHINESE CIVILIZATION HAS A LONG AND IMPRESSIVE HISTORY. By the 1800's, however, China had failed to develop modern industries and technology. After a series of small wars and rebellions, China lost territory to the United Kingdom and Japan. The spread of foreign customs and religion threatened many Chinese people. They blamed their rulers, the Qing emperors, for China's misfortunes. A revolution erupted and, in 1912, the last Qing emperor was removed from power. China became a *republic* (a country governed by an elected leader rather than an emperor), and the revolutionary leader Sun Yat-sen (1866-1925) became its first president. However, after just two months, Sun was forced from power by Yuan Shikai, a retired military official. Yuan died in 1916 and the government quickly lost control of the country, most of which became dominated by *warlords* (local military leaders).

◀ An imperial Chinese officer prepares to execute a revolutionary prisoner in 1912. After a series of bloody revolts, revolutionary troops won control of China, ending more than 2,000 years of imperial rule.

▶ China's education minister Fu Zengxiang responds to a student demonstration in Beijing on May 4, 1919. The students were protesting the decision to allow Japan to keep China's Shandong Province after World War I (1914-1918). Shandong had been controlled by Germany before the war. During the war, German holdings in China were seized by Japan. In return for China's support during the war, the Allies had promised to return Shandong to China. The "May Fourth Movement" became an important political and cultural force, and a key to the development of Chinese nationalism. Shandong was returned to China in 1922.

Today, at 1 p.m., two thousand students held a meeting to demonstrate against the government's diplomatic policies. This is a troublesome, unfortunate occurrence. To maintain public order and student discipline, we call upon all schools to assume prompt responsibility for the disorderly behavior of their students.

Education minister
Fu Zengxiang, 1919

▶ In a January 1924 speech, Sun Yat-sen argues that China needs a new nationalist spirit. Confucianism, an ancient Chinese philosophy, taught loyalty to family and clan. Sun felt that loyalty should extend to the nation as well. He believed a more modern and patriotic outlook would strengthen China.

What is nationalism? . . . nationalism is the doctrine of the state-nation. What Chinese people worship is the family and clan, so China only adheres [sticks] to the doctrines of the family and clan, not to the state-nation. . . . For Chinese, the unifying force of family and clan is very great indeed and many have been willing to sacrifice their families and lives to defend the clan. . . . But there has never been a case of such supreme sacrifice for the sake of the country.

Sun Yat-sen, 1924

◀ Zhongshan Road in the Bund, an area in the Chinese port of Shanghai. In 1842, China was forced by Britain to open Shanghai and other ports to foreign trade and settlement. The Bund was within the British settlement, and became the wealthiest area of the city. It housed numerous foreign banks and merchant offices in grand buildings like Sassoon House (left, with pyramidal roof).

NOW YOU KNOW

- More than 2,000 years of imperial rule in China ended in 1912.
- Sun Yat-sen became the first president of the Republic of China.
- By 1916, the republic had collapsed, and warlords controlled most of China.

China Divided

THE 1920'S BROUGHT POLITICAL CHANGE AND TURMOIL TO CHINA. Sun Yat-sen died in 1925, and General Chiang Kai-shek (1887-1975) gradually assumed leadership of Sun's Kuomintang (Nationalist Party). The rival Communist Party aimed to destroy the existing ruling class and put the working people in charge. At first, the Nationalists and Communists worked together to defeat the warlords. But in 1927, Chiang Kai-shek turned against the Communists, executing many members of Communist-backed labor unions. Surviving Communists fled to the hills, escaping to remote Shaanxi Province in what became known as the "Long March." During the march, more than 70,000 Communists soldiers died from combat, disease, and starvation, and Mao Zedong (1893-1976) emerged as leader of the Communist Party.

▶ The Communist fighting forces were called the Red Army because red is the color associated with Communism. In October 1934, the Red Army began a 6,000-mile (9,700-kilometer) retreat to escape the Nationalist army. Mao Zedong named the 368-day journey the "Long March." In this December 1935 speech, Mao describes the Long March as a heroic example of the Communists' toughness and determination.

▼ Mao Zedong on horseback during the Long March. Mao helped form the Chinese Communist Party in 1921, becoming its leader in 1935.

1

Let us ask, has history ever known a long march to equal ours? No, never. The Long March ... has proclaimed to the world that the Red Army is an army of heroes. ... The Long March ... has sown many seeds which will sprout, leaf, blossom, and bear fruit, and will yield a harvest in the future. In a word, the Long March has ended with victory for us and defeat for the enemy.

Mao Zedong, 1935

2

3

4

In the last few days' march, we did badly with our discipline . . . leaving straw bedding about, taking things from people without permission – this happens frequently. . . . People do not listen to our sweet talk; they observe our actions. An army without discipline will not win their sympathy and support, no matter how much propaganda we do.

Deng Xiaoping, 1934

▲ Deng Xiaoping (1904-1997) was secretary-general of the Communist Party and editor of the Communist newspaper *Red Star*. In this 1934 *Red Star* editorial, he revealed difficult times during the "Long March." Communist leaders struggled to maintain discipline among their starving and diseased troops. Deng Xiaoping himself nearly died of typhoid fever.

▲ Chinese Communist forces wind through Loushan Pass after having fought and won control of it from Nationalist forces. Mao Zedong wrote a poem to commemorate the Red Army victory.

NOW YOU KNOW

• During the 1920's and 1930's, the Nationalists and Communists struggled for control of China.

• The Communists lost thousands of soldiers on the Long March.

• Mao Zedong became leader of the Communist Party in 1935.

Conflict with Japan

IN 1931, JAPAN INVADED THE NORTHEASTERN CHINESE PROVINCE OF MANCHURIA. Chiang Kai-shek insisted on eliminating the Communists before fighting Japan, and Manchuria quickly fell to the Japanese. Nationalist troops from Manchuria who were blockading Communist-held areas opposed Chiang's lack of resistance to Japan. In 1936, the Manchurian forces kidnapped Chiang. He was released only after agreeing to end the civil war and form a united front against the Japanese. In 1937, Japan launched a full-scale invasion of China, overwhelming the Chinese and treating them with great brutality. Untold numbers of Chinese people died, including at least 100,000 in the eastern city of Nanjing (Nanking). By late 1938, Japan controlled most of eastern China.

1

We have been fighting each other ... for a dozen years. We should have a rest. We sincerely want to work with you to fight against the Japanese. This is the voice of the whole nation. You are patriotic and I'm sure you feel the same. ... If we can communicate with each other, you would reduce the losses to your troops, and preserve your strength to fight against the Japanese.

Mao Zedong, 1934

◄ Nearing the end of the Long March, Mao Zedong appealed to Nationalist generals to join him in the struggle against Japan. Mao appealed to Chinese patriotism, but a truce with the Nationalists also took pressure off his battered Communist army.

▼ Japanese propaganda posters were designed to convince Westerners of the happy life of newly free and independent Manchuria (Manchoukuo). After Japan's conquest of Manchuria, more than 300,000 Japanese farmers and their families settled on land taken from the Chinese.

2

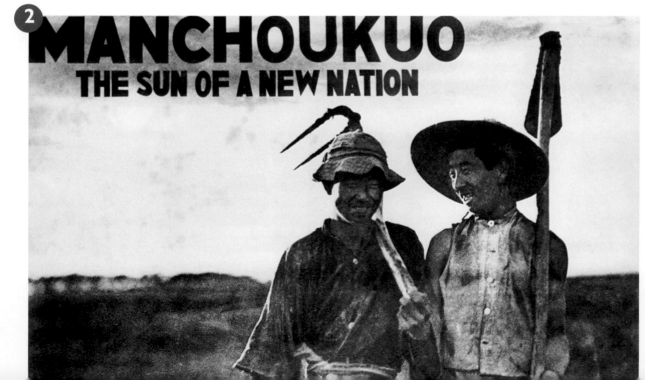

MANCHOUKUO
THE SUN OF A NEW NATION

3

... Of the seventeen people living in a small house near the end of the street where our old house used to be, six have been killed because they sank to their knees outside the house and begged the Japanese soldiers to spare their daughters. After the old people had been shot, the girls were dragged away. ... You can't breathe for sheer revulsion [disgust] when you keep finding the bodies of women ...

John Rabe
Nanjing, 1937

◀ German businessman John Rabe was in Nanjing when the Japanese captured it in December 1937. Rabe described the brutal actions of the conquering Japanese soldiers in his diary. At least 100,000 Chinese died in what became known as "the rape of Nanjing." Reports of Japanese cruelty created great sympathy for China around the world.

4

▶ A Chinese family grieves in the ruins of their home after a Japanese bombing raid. The city of Chongqing (Chungking) alone was bombed more than 5,000 times between 1938 and 1943.

NOW YOU KNOW

- In 1931, Japan invaded Manchuria in northeast China.
- In 1936, the Nationalists and Communists joined forces to fight the Japanese.
- By the end of 1938, Japan controlled much of eastern China.

China in World War II

IN 1939, GERMANY ATTACKED POLAND, BEGINNING WORLD WAR II IN EUROPE. In December 1941, Japan attacked United States forces in Hawaii, Guam, and Wake Island, and the war spread to the Far East. The war drew many Japanese troops from China. Japanese progress in China was halted, but fighting continued. The Nationalist government became increasingly *corrupt* (dishonest and unjust) and unpopular with the Chinese people. The Communists appealed more to the people and gained control of large areas of northern China as the war progressed.

They cannot take advantage of the hill country, but must follow the easiest and most level route . . . so we always fight in the hills, not in open country.

Zhu De

In the area of Hsin-hsiang, very small Japanese garrisons, of five to forty soldiers, occupy villages which are invested [besieged] by the numerically superior forces of [Communist commander] Ho Lung. I asked why they did not recapture the villages . . . [the men] admitted "We are told not to touch them." . . . As we could see, the Kuomintang forces are the main concern of the [Communists].

Peter Vladimirov, 1942

▲ Zhu De (1886-1976), a Red Army commander, describes how the Red Army used *guerrilla* warfare, striking the Japanese in unexpected places and then disappearing into the hills. Japan's modern army with tanks and artillery had to stick to the roads. The Communists, mostly peasants armed with rifles, moved swiftly in small groups.

▲ In a September 1942 diary entry, Peter Vladimirov, a Soviet advisor to the Chinese Communists, suggests that the Communists were more concerned with preparing to fight the Nationalists than with defeating the Japanese. The Chinese Communists claimed that this was untrue. Immediately after Japan's surrender in 1945, the Nationalists and Communists resumed their civil war.

3

I have never heard Chiang Kai-shek say a single thing that indicated [showed] gratitude to the President or to our country for the help we were extending to him. Invariably [always], when anything was promised, he would want more.... He would complain that the Chinese had been fighting for six or seven years and yet we gave them practically nothing. It would of course be undiplomatic [lacking in skill for handling sensitive matters] to go into the nature of the military effort Chiang Kai-shek had made since 1938. It was practically zero.

Joseph Stilwell

▲ U.S. Army General Joseph Stilwell (1883-1946) commanded the Allied forces in China early in the war. Stilwell complained of widespread corruption and a lack of training in the Chinese army. He also criticized Chiang Kai-shek's obsession with the Communists.

4

▲ A wartime propaganda poster glorifies General Chiang Kai-shek and the Chinese Nationalist army. The real army was not so well disciplined or equipped.

NOW YOU KNOW

- World War II spread to the Far East with Japan's December 1941 attack on Hawaii.
- The Nationalist government lost popularity with the Chinese people during the war.
- The Communists gained strength during the war, especially in northern China.

Showdown

IN 1945, THE UNITED STATES DROPPED ATOMIC BOMBS on the Japanese cities of Hiroshima and Nagasaki, forcing Japan to surrender. In 1946, full-scale civil war again erupted in China between the Nationalists and Communists after U. S. Army General George C. Marshall (1880-1959) failed to arrange a peace agreement. The United States helped the Nationalists, and the Soviet Union supplied the Communists. The Communists, however, used superior military tactics and had the support of China's peasant majority. By 1949, Communist victory was certain. In December, Chiang Kai-shek and his supporters fled to the Chinese island of Taiwan (Formosa).

1

The Three Rules:

Obey orders in all your actions

Do not take a single needle or thread from the masses

Turn in everything captured

The Eight Points:

Speak politely

Pay fairly for what you buy

Return everything you borrow

Pay for anything you damage

Do not hit or swear at people

Do not damage crops

Do not take liberties with women

Do not ill-treat captives

Mao Zedong, 1929

◀ Mao Zedong wrote the "Three Main Rules of Discipline and the Eight Points for Attention" for the Chinese Red Army during their struggles against the Kuomintang in 1929. To win popular support, Mao needed Communist troops to treat peasants with kindness and respect. Nationalist troops followed no such rules. They often acted cruelly and took whatever they needed from the peasants, making the Nationalist government highly unpopular.

2

The . . . [Nationalist] Government have evidently counted on substantial American support regardless of their action. The Communists by their unwillingness to compromise in the national interest are evidently counting on an economic collapse to bring about the fall of the Government, accelerated [speeded up] by extensive guerrilla action against the long lines of rail communications — regardless of the cost in suffering to the Chinese people.

George C. Marshall, 1947

▶ In January 1947, General George C. Marshall reported on his failure to make peace between the Nationalists and Communists. Marshall believed that neither side would put China's best interests above their own ambitions. Marshall served as chief of staff of the United States Army during World War II and as secretary of state from 1947 to 1949.

3

▲ Nationalist troops prepare for the defence of Shanghai as Communist forces approach the city in May 1949. Shanghai, China's largest and wealthiest city, quickly fell to the Communists. In October, Mao proclaimed the establishment of the People's Republic of China in Beijing, the new capital.

NOW YOU KNOW

- After the end of World War II, civil war erupted again in China between the Communists and Nationalists.
- George Marshall failed to make peace between the Communists and Nationalists.
- The Communists defeated the Nationalists in 1949, ending the civil war.

Founding the People's Republic

O N OCT. 1, 1949, COMMUNIST LEADER MAO ZEDONG addressed the Chinese people in Tiananmen Square, Beijing. Mao proclaimed the founding of a new Communist Chinese state, the People's Republic of China (PRC), with Beijing as its capital. Mao was chairman of the Communist Party, and Zhou Enlai (1898-1976) headed the government. The new government firmly established control over China and worked to rebuild the nation's shattered economy after decades of war. The PRC established relations with other Communist nations, including the Soviet Union, then the world's most powerful Communist country.

1

The Chinese have always been a great, courageous and industrious nation; it is only in modern times that they have fallen behind. And that was due entirely to oppression and exploitation by foreign . . . and domestic . . . governments. For over a century our forefathers never stopped waging unyielding struggles . . . including the Revolution of 1911 led by Dr. Sun Yat-sen, our great forerunner in the Chinese revolution . . . and now we are proclaiming the founding of the People's Republic of China.

Mao Zedong, 1949

◀ A Sept. 21, 1949, speech by Mao Zedong ties the Communist cause to Chinese national pride. He blamed China's long period of weakness on foreign interference and bad government. Mao portrayed the Communist victory as a triumph for the Chinese people and as the final step in the struggle begun by China's national hero, Sun Yat-sen.

▼ *Grand Ceremony of the Founding of the Nation* (1953), an oil painting by Dong Xiwen (1914-1973), depicts Chairman Mao proclaiming the founding of the PRC before thousands of Chinese gathered in Tiananmen Square in Beijing. Over the years, the painting was altered several times as various leaders in the painting went in and out of favor.

2

3

My comrades at arms,

My brothers,

I have seen you

Dying in a dank and stench-filled prison,

Starving and freezing in a deserted village.

You – you and the peasants – have fed lice
with your flesh,

Have drunk bloody water on the battlefield
with your friends.

You have endured repeated hammerings,
repeated trials.

You have conquered pain and death.

Hu Feng, 1949

◀ Hu Feng (1902–1985) celebrates the founding of the People's Republic of China in his 1949 poem, *Song of Joy*. It described the Red Army and its supporters in heroic terms, emphasizing their suffering for the cause. Hu Feng portrayed the creation of the People's Republic as a new beginning that would allow the Chinese people to put the painful past behind them.

▼ Mao Zedong (center left) in Moscow with Soviet leader Joseph Stalin (1879-1953, center) on Dec. 21, 1949–Stalin's 70th birthday. Mao hoped for substantial support for his new Communist republic, but Stalin offered little help.

4

NOW YOU KNOW

- The People's Republic of China was founded on Oct. 1, 1949.

- Beijing became the new capital of China.

- China allied itself with other Communist powers, including the Soviet Union

The New Government

THE NEW COMMUNIST GOVERNMENT brought land, industry, and wealth under state control. Nationalist Party property was seized, and the government took over China's banks and utilities (public services such as transportation). At first, some non-Communists and ex-Kuomintang officials were allowed to hold positions in the new government. Before long, however, China settled into a one-party state in which no opposition was allowed, and only Communist ideas could be published or broadcast.

1

In all the practical work of our Party, all correct leadership is necessarily "from the masses, to the masses". This means: take the ideas of the masses . . . and concentrate them (through study turn them into concentrated and systematic ideas), then go to the masses and . . . explain these ideas until the masses embrace them as their own.

Mao Zedong, 1943

◀ In Mao's 1943 pamphlet, "Some Questions Concerning Methods of Leadership," he explains how the Communist Party dictatorship was "democratic" because it drew its ideas from the masses (the majority of the people). Mao assumed that the Party would always understand what the masses wanted and work for the common good.

2

▶ People raise their fists in salute of victorious Chinese Communist forces entering Beijing on Feb. 5, 1949. The portraits are of Mao Zedong (center), General Lin Biao (1903-1971, left), and General Zhu De (right).

▶ American student Derk Bodde describes in *Peking Diary: A Year of Revolution* how the Communist Party controlled people's thoughts through propaganda and *censorship* (preventing opponents' ideas from being published or broadcast). Bodde later became a professor of Chinese at the University of Pennsylvania.

3

It is in . . . thought-control that we reach the most questionable aspect of the new program. The authorities are trying, with considerable success, to see that only their point of view reaches the people. Slogans and posters carrying their message now adorn [decorate] all public places. Many, painted in bright colors, are very effective, for example the one depicting a galloping cavalryman holding aloft a red banner, beneath which appears the caption: "Plant the victorious banner throughout China!" . . . Movies are now said to be subject to censorship. . . . Newspapers have suffered . . . at least seven having been closed in Peking [Beijing].

Derk Bodde, 1950

4

◀ Mao Zedong (in dark blue jacket), Liu Shaoqi (1898-1969, in red), and Zhou Enlai (in the long coat) meet with generals of the People's Liberation Army. Throughout China, murals and posters showed images of Communist leaders and soldiers in heroic and idealized poses.

NOW YOU KNOW

- The new government brought land, industry, and wealth under state control.
- The Communists set up a one-party state in which no opposition was allowed.
- Propaganda and censorship were used to influence people's thoughts.

China Expands

THE COMMUNIST GOVERNMENT SOON EXPANDED CHINA'S BORDERS. In 1949 and 1950, Chinese armies moved into two far western regions, Xinjiang and Tibet. Although these regions had once been part of China, they had their own different local traditions and ethnic backgrounds. Xinjiang, then part of an independent republic, had no standing army to resist the Communists. The top leaders of the region were killed and replaced. Tibet, then an independent state, had a small army that was quickly overwhelmed by Red Army forces. Tibet's religious leaders, the Dalai Lama (1935-) and Panchen Lama (1938-1989), worked with the Chinese to avoid further violence.

1

The Chinese People's Liberation Army must liberate the whole territory of China, including Tibet, Xinjiang and so forth. Even an inch of Chinese land will not be permitted to be left outside the jurisdiction of the People's Republic of China. We tolerate no longer the aggression of the foreign countries. This is the unchangeable policy of the Chinese Communist Party and the Chinese People's Liberation Army.

Hsin Hwa Pao, Sept. 2, 1949

◀ The editors of the Beijing newspaper *Hsin Hwa Pao* express the Communists' determination to recover all territories that had once belonged to China. After more than a century of foreign interference in China, the Chinese felt justified in reclaiming Xinjiang and Tibet. To much of the world, however, the occupations were seen as acts of aggression against weaker neighbors.

2

▶ Chinese troops make a difficult river crossing during the 1950 invasion of Tibet. The Chinese government called it a "peaceful liberation," but thousands of Tibetans and Chinese lost their lives.

3

> While most officials live smugly in their ivory towers [away from reality] . . . the common people find the heavy burdens imposed on them insupportable [unbearable]. For them Communism in practice has fallen far short of expectations, and they have derived little comfort from the alliance which the Communists have forged with the ruling aristocracy of Tibet. In complete disenchantment, they ask whether this is "liberation."
>
> S. Sinha, March 1952

◀ A 1952 report to the government of India by S. Sinha, the Indian representative in Tibet, describes the failure of Communism to win over the Tibetan people. Rising food prices and a shortage of supplies and medicine led to widespread hunger and disease.

▼ Mao Zedong (center) meets with the Dalai Lama (second from right) and Panchen Lama (second from left) in Beijing in 1956. The Communists and traditional Tibetan leaders tried hard to cooperate, but troubles continued.

4

NOW YOU KNOW

- The Chinese Red Army invaded and took control of Xinjiang and Tibet in 1949 and 1950.
- The way of life and religions in these regions were different from those in most of China.
- Troubles continued in Tibet despite the efforts of Chinese and Tibetan leaders.

Early Reforms

IN 1950, THE COMMUNIST GOVERNMENT BEGAN A PROGRAM OF LAND REFORM. In China, many wealthy landlords had mistreated their peasant laborers. Communist promises to end landlord control had won the Party wide support. Officials held village meetings, forcing the landlords to attend. The peasants were encouraged to describe, even invent, how they had been mistreated. The landlords were often beaten and killed, and their property was then divided among the villagers. Angry mobs, resentful of the way they had been mistreated, killed at least 200,000 landlords. Before long, the land that had been given to the peasants was returned to the state.

▶ A peasant describes the treatment of a landlord named Ching-ho to American writer William Hinton during the period of land reform. The peasants took revenge on Ching-ho after years of mistreatment.

①

That evening all the people went to Ching-ho's courtyard to help take over his property. . . . We went in to register his grain and altogether found but [only] 200 bags. . . . We called him out of the house and asked him what he intended to do since the grain was not nearly enough. He said, "I have land and house." "But all this is not enough," shouted the people. So then we began to beat him. Finally he said, "I have 40 silver dollars." . . . We went in and dug it up. The money stirred up everyone. We beat him again. . . . Altogether we got $500 from Ching-ho that night.

Fanshen: A Documentary of Revolution in a Chinese Village, 1966

②

◀ Happy Chinese peasants gather rice in the fields. Although photographs like this were often posed, most poor peasants were grateful to receive their own land.

3

It was very cold that day. Everyone was saying: "How cold! There must be quite a few frozen to death today. What have we done to deserve this!" . . . After careful rehearsals, on the fifth day denunciations [accusations against the landlords] began . . . the masses were told to raise their weapons when the word was given and [the] shout . . . "Kill! Kill! Kill!" . . . the rally site was in a chaotic storm, and ended in eight people being beaten to death.

Mao Anying, 1950

◀ Mao Zedong's oldest son, Mao Anying (1922-1950), describes land reform in his diary. He was disturbed by the brutal way it was carried out. Anying noted that accusations against the landlords were sometimes made up or exaggerated and that events were carefully planned. Anying also noticed that some of the Communist officials enjoyed the violence.

▶ In a Land Reform era painting, angry farmers accuse a landlord of abuses. The farmers fly the red banner of Communism. The landlord is shown as well-fed, to emphasize his privileged life and laziness.

4

NOW YOU KNOW

- The Communists introduced land reform throughout China in 1950.
- At least 200,000 landlords were killed.
- The peasants welcomed land reform.

The Korean War

I N 1945, KOREA WAS DIVIDED INTO TWO STATES. North Korea, like China, was a Communist state. South Korea was a democracy. On June 25, 1950, North Korea invaded South Korea. Forces of the United Nations (UN)—mostly from the United States—arrived to help the South Koreans. The UN troops pushed the North Koreans all the way back near the Chinese border. Mao Zedong then sent troops to help the North Koreans. The UN forces retreated and formed a battle line that moved little over the next two years. When the fighting ended in July 1953, the original border between North and South Korea was nearly unchanged.

▶ Mao Zedong orders Chinese volunteers into action on Oct. 8, 1950. He made the decision to intervene in Korea as UN forces approached the Chinese border. More than 300,000 Chinese troops crossed into North Korea in October and November.

1

In order to support the Korean people's war of liberation and to resist the attacks of U.S. imperialism [aggressive empire-building] . . . thereby safeguarding the interests of the people of Korea, China and all the other countries in the East, I herewith order the Chinese People's Volunteers to march speedily to Korea and join the Korean comrades in fighting the aggressors and winning a glorious victory.

Order to the Chinese
People's Volunteers, 1950

▼Soldiers of the U.S. 1st Marine Division take Chinese prisoners in Korea in 1951. Hundreds of thousands of Chinese troops were killed in the Korean War, including Mao Anying—the son of Mao Zedong—on Nov. 25, 1950.

2

3

This is certainly no time for optimism. It's mean and nasty. . . . Still sleep with our boots on. When we do sleep it's only for a few moments. . . . The battalion has been fortunate that so far the [enemy] haven't hit us. I'm told the enemy is well trained and organized. They speak Chinese and were born and raised in China; they'd never heard of Korea before now.

Norman Allen, 1950

◀ U.S. Army Captain Norman Allen describes some of his Korean War experiences in a letter to his mother on Nov. 4, 1950. Allen's company had first engaged Chinese soldiers earlier in the day.

4

▶ Chinese students rally in support of North Korea in 1953. The Communist government organized such rallies to boost popular enthusiasm for the war. A South Korean victory was portrayed as a threat to China.

NOW YOU KNOW

- North Korea invaded South Korea in 1950.
- The United States and its UN allies fought on the side of South Korea and China fought on the side of North Korea.
- The Korean War ended in 1953, leaving the border between North and South Korea very little changed.

Taiwan

AFTER THEIR DEFEAT BY THE COMMUNISTS, CHIANG KAI-SHEK and the Nationalists fled to Taiwan (Formosa), an island 90 miles (140 kilometers) off the Chinese coast. On Dec. 8, 1949, Chiang declared Taipei, a city at the northern end of Taiwan, capital of the Republic of China. After the Korean War began in 1950, the United States protected Taiwan against possible attack from Communist China. With economic, military, and technical aid from the United States, Taiwan enjoyed steadily increasing economic success. Chiang, who ruled as a dictator, dealing viciously with opponents, remained in power until his death in 1975.

1

The present methods adopted by the Kuomintang government are . . . directly contrary to the fundamental principles of modern democratic government. . . . During my more than three years' administration . . . hardly a day passed without some bitter struggle on my part with the secret police. They interfered with free elections. They made numberless illegal arrests. They tortured and they blackmailed . . . Formosa has become virtually a police state. The liberties of the people are almost totally suppressed.

Wu Kuo-chen
Feb. 27, 1954

◀ Wu Kuo-chen (1903-1984) writes to Chiang Kai-shek on Feb. 27, 1954, criticizing the Nationalist government. Wu had been governor of Taiwan from 1949 until an attempt on his life in 1953. He then fled to the United States and wrote a highly critical article for *Look* magazine entitled "Your Money is Building a Police State in Taiwan."

2

▶ The American warship *USS Manchester* sails into the Taiwan Straits in 1950 as part of the U.S. Naval force sent to prevent war between Taiwan and the PRC.

3

For among the foxes of the world, Chiang Kai-shek long ago found the hedgehog's one big thing: the world's primary . . . enemy was and is the Communist conspiracy directed from Moscow. It was a single-mindedness that in the 1930s exasperated [annoyed] his countrymen (who wanted him to fight Japanese instead of Communists). . . . While many bright young foxes were finding that the grapes were bitter, Chiang Kai-shek, who himself has erred grievously in other things . . . clung to his hedgehog truth.

Time
April 18, 1955

◀ *Time* magazine recalls a Chinese fable: the fox knows many things, but the hedgehog knows one big thing. Many people saw Chiang's "one big thing" as his opposition to Communism. The Cold War—the intense rivalry that developed after World War II between groups of Communist and non-Communist nations—blinded many people, including *Time*'s founder, Henry Luce, to the fact that Chiang Kai-shek was a dictator.

4

▶ A statue of Chiang Kai-shek in the main vault of the Chiang Kai-shek Memorial Hall. The memorial opened in Taipei's Liberty Square on April 5, 1980—exactly five years after his death. Some Taiwanese people continue to view Chiang as a hero; others regard him with hatred. In the years since his death, hundreds of his statues have been removed from public spaces.

NOW YOU KNOW

- The Nationalists, headed by Chiang Kai-shek, fled to Taiwan in 1949.
- Chiang ruled the Republic of China as a dictator.
- With aid from the United States, Taiwan's economy flourished.

Dealing with Dissent

UNDER COMMUNIST RULE, DISSENT—disagreement and opposition to the Party—was not allowed. By 1952, all other political parties had ceased to exist. Political opponents were arrested and sent to slave labor camps where they were often starved and tortured. Citizens were encouraged to spy on one another and report behavior disloyal to the Communist government. Then in 1956, Mao switched direction and launched the Hundred Flowers Movement "letting a hundred flowers bloom and a hundred schools of thought contend." The campaign encouraged debate on national policy issues. This opportunity for free speech resulted in so much criticism of Communist rule that the experiment was ended in 1958. Hundreds of thousands of people who spoke out against the government were imprisoned.

1

The grass and beaten earth huts we lived in had wind coming in from all sides . . . there were hardly any vegetables or meat. . . . We got up . . . just after 4 at dawn, and did not stop until 7 or 8 in the evening. . . . In these 15–16 hours . . . we basically worked non-stop . . . in summer . . . we had to get up at 2 a.m. . . . We had at most three hours' sleep.

Dai Huang, 1998

◀ Dai Huang, in his book *A Narrow Escape From Death* (1998), describes his 21 years in a slave labor camp. In 1957, Dai was imprisoned during the Hundred Flowers Movement for criticizing Mao and the Communist government. He was finally released in 1978. Many development projects throughout China depended upon slave labor. The camps were often located in the harshest regions of China, and prisoners were forced to do exhausting work. Food was scarce, and many people starved to death.

2

▶ Beijing university student Lin Xiling speaks out against the methods of the Chinese Communist Party in a 1957 speech. A true socialist, Lin believed in the common good. She argued that the Party cared only about keeping power. She said one-party rule is undemocratic and gives the people no voice in government. Lin was arrested soon after her speech and imprisoned from 1958 until 1983. She fled to France upon her release.

I believe that public ownership is better than private ownership, but I hold that the socialism we now have is not genuine socialism. . . . Genuine socialism should be very democratic, but ours is undemocratic . . . we must struggle for genuine socialism!

Lin Xiling, 1957

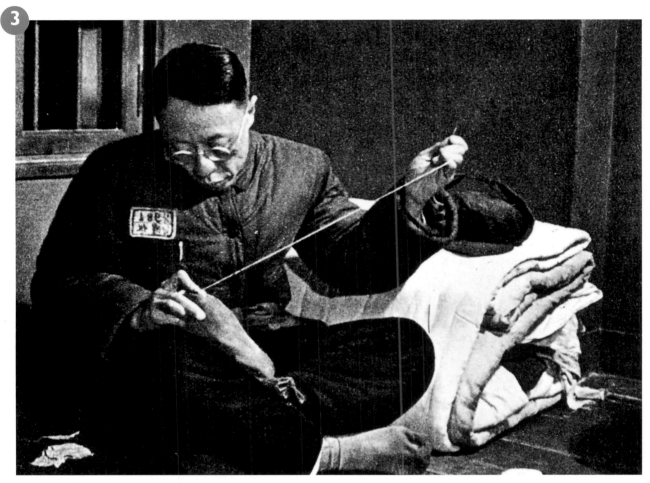

▲ Pu Yi (1906-1967), the last emperor of China, mends socks in prison in the 1950's. Pu Yi lost the throne in 1912 when he was still a child. From 1934 to 1945, he served as Japan's puppet ruler of the Japanese-controlled state of Manchukuo (Manchuria). The Chinese Communists imprisoned Pu Yi in 1950. After his release in 1959, he worked as a gardener and editor until his death in 1967.

NOW YOU KNOW

- The Chinese Communist Party did not allow dissent.
- The Hundred Flowers Movement encouraged people to voice their opinions, but many of those who did were arrested.
- Opponents of the Communist government were often imprisoned for years in slave labor camps.

The Great Leap Forward

IN 1958, MAO ZEDONG LAUNCHED A FIVE-YEAR PLAN CALLED THE GREAT LEAP FORWARD. The plan was intended to transform China into an advanced industrialized nation. Much farmland had already been organized into cooperatives—groups of farmers who shared everything and worked the land together. With the new plan, private land was abolished completely, and the farming cooperatives were organized into giant communes, or groups of collective farms. In the cities, factory laborers worked long hours, often sleeping at their machines. Mao wanted China to produce enough crops and steel to compete with the United Kingdom and, eventually, the United States.

1

When the communes were first set up, it was real communism. The mess hall was great. We got to eat things made from wheat flour every day, and they were always slaughtering pigs for us. For a while it seemed that they were telling the truth and we were going to enter heaven. No one would have believed you if you had suggested that the Communist Party had got it all wrong. . . . They said that "Communism is heaven, and the communes are the bridge that will take us there." We felt like we were crossing that bridge, could heaven really be far away?

A high school student
1960

◀ In a 1995 interview with an historian, a Chinese man recalls his early experiences as an agricultural high school student on a commune. Many people believed the Party's promises and expected the communes to bring a new era of good harvests, equality, and personal freedom.

2

▶ A poster portrays Chairman Mao walking through a fertile field during the Great Leap Forward. The Chinese reads "The People's Communes are Good!" Tens of thousands of people might belong to a single commune. Everyone worked and ate together. In some places, communal barracks took the place of individual farm houses.

人民公社好

我们的伟大领袖毛主席，在大跃进的一九五八年巡视大江南北。

28

3

> The spring of 1958 witnessed the beginning of a leap forward on every front in our socialist construction. Industry, agriculture and all other fields of activity are registering greater and more rapid growth.
>
> Liu Shaoqi, 1958

▲ Communist Vice Chairman Liu Shaoqi greatly exaggerates the success of the Great Leap Forward in a 1958 report to the national Congress. Liu privately doubted the wisdom of the plan and later helped correct its failures. All Communists had to follow the "party line," supporting official policies even when they disagreed with them.

▶ Female workers at an electric motor factory in 1960 are shown how to operate machinery. Under Communism, Chinese women often took jobs traditionally held by men.

4

NOW YOU KNOW

- In 1958, Mao launched the Great Leap Forward, a plan to increase China's productivity.
- Agriculture was organized into enormous group farms called communes.
- Industrial employees worked very long hours.

A Great Leap Backward

THE GREAT LEAP FORWARD WAS A DISASTER FOR CHINA. From 1959 to 1961, China suffered economic depression, food shortages, and a decline in industrial output. In an effort to produce more food faster, the government forced peasants to use new techniques that did not work. Farmers using traditional methods risked imprisonment and torture. Many farm workers were sent from the countryside to work in the cities, leaving a shortage of people to harvest what food was produced. During this period, more than 30 million Chinese people starved to death. The failures of the Great Leap Forward caused Mao Zedong to retire as chairman of the People's Republic of China in 1959. He remained chairman of the Communist Party.

1

◀ Mao Zedong turns a shovel for a photographer at the Ming Tombs Reservoir in Beijing in May 1958. Such photos suggested that even the most important Communist leaders did their share of work. During the winters and springs of the Great Leap Forward, ordinary citizens built reservoirs and irrigation channels, dug wells, and dredged river bottoms.

2

The exaggeration trend has become so common in various areas and departments that reports of unbelievable miracles have appeared in newspapers. . . . According to what was reported, it seemed that communism was just around the corner. . . . Extravagance and waste grew in the wake of reports of extra-large grain and cotton harvests and a doubling of iron and steel output. As a result . . . though we were poor, we lived as if we were rich.
Peng Dehuai, 1959

▶ Defense minister Peng Dehuai (1898-1974) writes to Mao outlining some of the problems of the Great Leap Forward during the 1959 Lushan Conference. Production was greatly exaggerated to please the Communist authorities. Because the figures were falsely high, grain was sold abroad even as people starved in China. Peng was a hero of the revolution, the war with Japan, and the Korean War, but his honesty cost him his job and, later, his life.

3

▶ Wei Wu-ji, a peasant leader, describes the effects of the famine on his commune in Anwei Province. The Great Leap Forward had brutal effects on the people of China, especially in poor areas. Wei's account was given to investigators sent by the Communist Party.

Originally there were 5,000 people in our commune, now only 3,200 remain. When the Japanese invaded we did not lose this many: we at least could save ourselves by running away! This year there's no escape. We die shut up in our own houses. Of my 6 family members, 5 are already dead, and I am left to starve, and I'll not be able to stave off death for long.
Wei Wu-ji, 1961

4

◀ Peasants work a blast furnace on a rural commune. These home-made furnaces were meant to produce steel, reducing the government's need for imported steel. Most of the metal created was, however, unuseable, and the project was a complete failure.

NOW YOU KNOW

- The failures of the Great Leap Forward resulted in the deaths of more than 30 million Chinese.
- New farming and steel production techniques did not work.
- Because of failed experiments, Mao Zedong retired as chairman of the People's Republic of China in 1959.

Troubles in Tibet

I N 1959, A REVOLT AGAINST CHINESE RULE ERUPTED IN THE TIBETAN CAPITAL OF LHASA. A suspected Chinese plot to kidnap the Dalai Lama sparked violent protests. The Dalai Lama is the leader of an important spiritual line of Tibetan Buddhist monks. Tibetan rebels barracaded themselves inside the Potala Palace, the Dalai Lama's residence, and in the surrounding streets. The Dalai Lama escaped to India two days before Chinese troops stormed the palace on March 19. Thousands of people were killed. The Chinese accused the Dalai Lama of plotting the revolt and broke the power of the Tibetan nobles. The local government was dissolved, and land reforms and other Communist policies were forced upon the Tibetan people.

▶ Chinese Communists are portrayed as democratic, liberating heroes in a Communist publication from 1977. Chinese forces entered Tibet in 1950, and Tibetan representatives signed an agreement with China in 1951 in which Tibet surrendered its *sovereignty* (self rule) to the Chinese government but kept its right to regional self-government. Tibetan society had been feudal, meaning that it was run by nobles and monks who dominated the peasants. Few Tibetans, however, welcomed Chinese rule, which was harsh and sparked the 1959 uprising.

> Under the guidance of Chairman Mao's *proletarian* [working people's] revolutionary line, Tibet was peacefully liberated in 1951, the armed rebellion in 1959 by the Dalai traitorous *clique* [group] was swiftly *quelled* [stopped], and the Democratic Reform that destroyed the feudal serf system followed closely in its wake . . . Tibet has advanced from feudal serfdom direct to a flourishing socialist society in less than two decades since the Democratic Reform.
>
> *Tibet Leaps Forward*, 1977

▼ Thousands of Tibetans gather in front of the Potala Palace on March 10, 1959, to defend the Dalai Lama from a possible Chinese kidnapping. Violent clashes erupted between the Tibetans and the Chinese, forcing the Dalai Lama into permanent exile.

3

Our *Han* [ethnic Chinese] *cadres* [Communist agents] produced a plan, our Tibetan cadres mobilized. . . . They *usurped* [took over] the name of the masses, they put on the mask of the masses. . . . They burned countless statues of the Buddha . . . threw them into the water, threw them onto the ground, broke them and melted them. Recklessly, they carried out a wild and hasty destruction of monasteries, halls, *mani* walls [walls built from prayer stones] . . . and stole many ornaments from the statues and precious things.

The Panchen Lama, May 1962

◀ The Panchen Lama, Tibetan Buddhism's second highest leader, details the failures of Chinese government policies in Tibet in a 1962 report to Chinese government officials. Unlike the Dalai Lama, the Panchen Lama remained in Tibet and cooperated with the Chinese. He tried to influence Communist policies to help Tibetans. By the time of this report, much of Tibet's cultural heritage had been destroyed.

▼ Tibetan rebels march out of the Potala Palace to surrender on May 9, 1959. The orderly photograph gives no hint of the massive loss of life and the destruction and damage from the fighting.

4

NOW YOU KNOW

- The Chinese took control of Tibet in 1951.
- The Dalai Lama escaped to India after a failed revolt against Chinese rule in March 1959.
- The Panchen Lama worked with the Communists, trying to improve conditions in Tibet.
- After the revolt, the Chinese forced Communist policies upon the Tibetan people.

China Begins to Recover

ALTHOUGH MAO ZEDONG HAD RETIRED AS CHAIRMAN OF THE PEOPLE'S REPUBLIC OF CHINA, he remained in control of the country and the Communist Party. With new ideas needed to rescue the country from the horrors of the Great Leap Forward, two leading Communists emerged: Liu Shaoqi and Deng Xiaoping. The two disagreed with some of Mao's stricter policies and encouraged a slight opening of markets. Millions of peasants who had been recruited to be industrial workers were sent back to the countryside. Some private farming was allowed again, enabling farmers to work for themselves and sell some of their produce. The situation began to improve, but Liu, Deng, and many others were later punished for their opposition to Mao.

▶ Chairman Liu Shaoqi reports to a Communist conference early in 1962. Although Mao Zedong and other leaders were ready to accept some blame, too much criticism was still dangerous. Liu fell out of favor with Mao after this report. Liu disappeared in 1968 and died from lack of medical attention the following year.

1

In the past several years many shortcomings and mistakes have occurred in our work. The cadres [Communist agents] and members of the whole Party and even the great majority of the people all have had personal painful experience of this. They have starved for two years.

Liu Shaoqi, 1962

▼ Starving people languish in a Chinese street, the result of policies put in place during the Great Leap Forward. By 1962, after new government policies returned farmers to the land and broke up the communes, food production began to improve throughout the country.

2

▶ Deng Xiaoping tells the Communist Youth League in a 1962 speech that strict adherance to Communist theory had brought famine and economic depression to China. Deng suggests allowing other methods, wherever they might work best, including private ownership and trading. Communist conservatives later used this speech to remove Deng from power for "going capitalist."

As to what kind of [means] of production is the best mode, I'm afraid we shall have to leave the matter to the . . . local authorities, allowing them to adopt whatever mode of production that can facilitate [make easier] the quickest recovery and growth of agricultural production. . . . At present, it looks as though neither industry nor agriculture can advance without first taking one step back.
Deng Xiaoping, 1962

◀ Mao Zedong (second from right) meets with other Communist leaders in Beijing in 1962. Liu Shaoqi (center) took over as chairman of the People's Republic of China in 1959. Liu's more liberal policies helped China recover from the disastrous Great Leap Forward.

NOW YOU KNOW

- Although Mao Zedong had officially retired as chairman, he still dominated Chinese politics.
- New, more liberal policies helped launch China's recovery from the Great Leap Forward.
- Liu Shaoqi and Deng Xiaoping masterminded China's recovery, but they were later punished for their opposition to Mao.

Break with the Soviet Union

MAO ALLIED CHINA WITH THE SOVIET UNION, THE STRONGEST COMMUNIST NATION in the world. Soviet dictator Joseph Stalin died in 1953. Unlike Mao and Stalin, the new Soviet leader, Nikita Khrushchev (1894-1971), believed his country could achieve a "peaceful coexistence" with Western powers like the United Kingdom and United States. As China still believed in an all-out "war against the imperialists," this easing of tensions with the West soured the relationship between China and the Soviet Union. The Soviets refused to share nuclear technology with China, and Khrushchev and Mao publicly denounced each other in 1960. Their alliance and diplomatic relations formally ended in 1964.

▲ Khrushchev and Mao exchange a toast during a meeting in Beijing in October 1959. Despite the smiles, relations between the two leaders and their countries were already tense. Khrushchev had denounced Stalin's violent, ruthless rule and his "cult of personality," which portrayed him as a godlike leader—very much as Mao was portrayed in China.

2

[The Communist leaders of the Soviet Union] are abusing their powers over the means of production and of livelihood for the private benefit of their small clique. The members . . . *appropriate* [take for themselves] the fruits of the Soviet people's labor and pocket incomes that are dozens or even a hundred times those of the average Soviet worker and peasant. . . . Completely divorced from the working people of the Soviet Union, they live the *parasitical* [exploitative] . . . life of the *bourgeoisie* [wealthy class].

People's Daily, 1964

◄ A July 14, 1964, edition of the *People's Daily,* the official mouthpiece of the Chinese Communist Party, attacks Khrushchev and the Soviet Communist Party. The editors describes Khrushchev as a "phoney Communist" straying from the ideals and goals of true Communism. In October 1964, Khrushchev was deposed by Leonid Brezhnev (1906-1982), who held on to power until his death.

3

► Chinese Foreign Minister Chen Yi (1901-1972) analyzes Stalin's record in a 1966 newspaper interview. Like Mao, Chen considered Stalin's killings and cult of personality unimportant. Chen believed Stalin's great mistake was his failure to erase capitalist and intellectual thought. Chen thought this made the Soviet Union vulnerable to *revisionism* (adapting Communist doctrines to changing national needs) and, eventually, capitalism.

At the Twentieth Party Congress, Khrushchev said that Stalin had killed many people. That's not important. That he had stimulated [encouraged] the cult of personality. That's secondary. Maybe Stalin made these mistakes. But there was a more serious one. . . He did not take steps to eliminate the capitalist evils . . . Stalin did not foresee the possibility of a turn toward capitalism. Because of this, the Soviet people were not prepared to confront [face and fight] revisionism.

Chen Yi, 1966

NOW YOU KNOW

- Soviet leader Nikita Khrushchev believed in a peaceful coexistence between East and West.
- Mao Zedong and other Chinese leaders accused Khrushchev and the Soviets of slipping from true Communist doctrine.
- China and the Soviet Union formally broke ties in 1964.

The Cultural Revolution

IN 1966, MAO RETOOK FORMAL CONTROL OF CHINA and launched a new movement: the Cultural Revolution. Acting against Chairman Liu Shaoqi and General Secretary Deng Xiaoping, Mao meant to enforce strict Communist principles while ridding China of his political opponents and *revisionists* (persons who advocate adapting Communist doctrines to changing national needs). Supporting Mao, radical party members accused many top officials of failing to follow Communist ideals. Liu, Deng, and others lost their positions, were arrested, tortured, or killed. *Maoism*, or Mao Zedong Thought, became the guide to all so-called revolutionary activity. The Cultural Revolution wrecked the Chinese government, economy, and education system so thoroughly that Mao had to call out the army to restore order in 1967.

1

In our great motherland, a new era is emerging in which the workers, peasants and soldiers are grasping Marxism–Leninism [Communist theory], Mao Zedong's thought. Once Mao Zedong's thought is grasped by the broad masses, it becomes an inexhaustible source of strength and a spiritual atom bomb of infinite power. The large-scale publication of *Quotations from Chairman Mao Zedong* is a vital measure for enabling the broad masses to grasp Mao Zedong's thought and for promoting the revolutionization of our people's thinking.

Lin Biao, 1967

◀ In the foreword of *Quotations from Chairman Mao Zedong*, Defense Minister Lin Biao describes the collection as a kind of Communist Bible. The "Little Red Book" became required reading for virtually every Chinese citizen. Those caught without a copy were often beaten. By December 1967, more than 350 million copies had been printed. More than 5 billion were eventually published.

最高指示

▶ In a propaganda poster, Mao surveys masses of loyal Chinese in Tiananmen Square essentially worshipping him. Posters like this, showing a god-like Mao, were put up everywhere in China during the Cultural Revolution.

2

伟大的领袖 英雄的人民

3

... My father is really the No. 1 Party person in authority taking the capitalist road. For more than twenty years, he has all the time opposed Chairman Mao and Mao's Thought, carrying out not socialism but capitalism.

Liu Tau, 1966

◀ The young daughter of Chairman Liu Shaoqi joins the attacks on her father in 1965. During this period, people in China denounced friends and family members out of fear. Others did so out of radical loyalty to Mao and the Cultural Revolution.

4

▶ Young students read from Mao's Little Red Book. The quoatations were accepted as gospel by Chinese youth—Mao's biggest supporters. During this period, "revolution" replaced much economic and educational activity in China.

NOW YOU KNOW

- In 1966, Mao returned to the center of Chinese politics.
- The Little Red Book was required reading for most Chinese citizens.
- The Cultural Revolution devastated China.

Red Guard Terror

THE CULTURAL REVOLUTION ENCOURAGED YOUTHFUL REBELLION and the abandonment of traditional principles. Millions of students joined violent, military-style groups called the Red Guards. The Red Guards enforced the ideals of the revolution, abusing, attacking, and often killing anyone they considered "counter-revolutionary." Unpopular teachers, officials, intellectuals, and artists fell victim to the *fanatical* (unreasonably enthusiastic) Red Guards. Mao pressed these gangs to destroy the "four olds" of pre-Communist China: old culture, old customs, old habits, and old ideas. Artwork, books, buildings, and ancient artifacts and shrines were destroyed. Mao and other radical Communist leaders claimed this mass destruction and violence was necessary for revolutionary advancement. The chaos also solidified their power.

▶ Minister of Public Security Xie Fuzhi (1909-1972) plainly states in a 1966 speech the government's approval of Red Guard violence. Police forces throughout China were powerless to stop the rampaging mobs.

1

Should Red Guards who kill people be punished? My view is that if people are killed, they are killed; it's no business of ours. . . . If the masses hate bad people so much that we cannot stop them, then let us not insist. . . . The people's police should stand on the side of the Red Guards, liaise [connect] with them, sympathize with them, and provide them with information, especially about the five black categories — the landlords, rich peasants, counter-revolutionaries, bad elements and Rightists.

Xie Fuzhi, 1966

2

◀ Mao gleams upon his adoring citizens in a Cultural Revolution-era poster. Propaganda promoted Mao's cult of personality, encouraging the Chinese people to worship and obey him like a god.

3

I saw . . . teachers standing on the platform on the sports ground, with their heads bent and their arms twisted into the "jet plane" position. Then, some were . . . forced to kneel, while others, including my English-language teacher, an elderly man . . . were forced to stand on long, narrow benches. He found it hard to keep his balance, and swayed and fell, cutting his forehead. . . . A Red Guard standing next to him instinctively stooped and extended his hands to help, but immediately straightened up . . . with his fists clenched, yelling: "Get back onto the bench!" He did not want to be seen as soft on a "class enemy."

Jung Chang

◄ Author Jung Chang (1952-) remembers the violence of the Cultural Revolution in her 1991 best-seller autobiography, *Wild Swans*. People showing sympathy to victims of the Red Guards were punished for a lack of revolutionary spirit.

4

► Red Guards parade a man though the streets in a dunce's hat. The Red Guards abused supposed enemies of the people in a variety of humiliating and painful ways.

NOW YOU KNOW

- Mao wanted to erase all evidence of pre-Communist China.
- Propaganda encouraged the people to worship Mao like a god.
- The Red Guards were allowed to attack "counter-revolutionaries."

Mao Triumphant

THE CULTURAL REVOLUTION REMOVED NEARLY ALL OPPOSITION TO MAO ZEDONG. Mao's enemies were disgraced, imprisoned, or killed. Not long after unleashing the Red Guards, however, Mao needed the People's Liberation Army (PLA) to stop the terror. The PLA, led by Defense Minister Lin Biao, took control, and the Red Guards were sent off to work in the countryside. In April 1969, Lin was designated to succeed Mao as chairman of the Chinese Communist Party. But soon Lin too came under suspicion. In September 1971, Lin died in an airplane crash in Mongolia. He was reportedly fleeing China after failing in an attempt to kill Mao and overthrow the government. Mao stood alone.

1

At six o'clock in the morning, the bugle call got people up, and they had twenty minutes to brush their teeth and have a wash. They then stood before the portrait of the Great Leader on the wall to seek "morning instructions," sang songs from Mao's Sayings, and, holding high the little red book, shouted out "long live" three times before going to the dining room to drink gruel. Assembly followed, and Mao's *Selected Works* were recited for half an hour before people shouldered their hoes and pickaxes to work on the land.

Gao Xingjian, 1999

◀ Nobel Prize winning author Gao Xingjian (1940–) describes the morning routine of paying homage to Mao during the Cultural Revolution in his fictionalized memoir, *One Man's Bible* (1999). The ceremony was remarkably similar to the worship of a god, showing the extraordinary position achieved by Mao as a result of the Cultural Revolution.

2

毛主席和林彪同志在天安门上检阅百万文化革命大军

▶ Mao Zedong and Lin Biao observe a rally in Beijing in 1966. Lin had worked closely with Mao since the Long March of 1934-1935. Lin won victories over Japanese invaders in the 1930's and over Nationalist armies in China's civil war. Lin and Mao's long partnership ended abruptly in 1971.

3

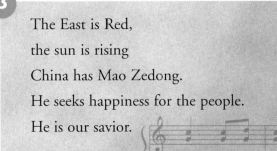

The East is Red,

the sun is rising

China has Mao Zedong.

He seeks happiness for the people.

He is our savior.

◀ "The East is Red" was an anthem of the Cultural Revolution. The song celebrating Mao was played before all important public events. It was also played each morning in schools, on the radio, and in the streets over loudspeakers.

▼ Chinese troops and officials stand over the corpses of executed Chinese citizens. Mao's government executed hundreds of thousands of people for a variety of reasons.

4

NOW YOU KNOW

- Mao used the Cultural Revolution to eliminate his political opponents and enemies.
- Lin Biao was chosen as Mao's successor but was killed in 1971.
- The Chinese government forced the worship of Mao into schools and people's homes.

Censorship

THE CHINESE COMMUNIST GOVERNMENT HEAVILY CENSORED EVERYTHING its citizens said, heard, wrote, read, saw, and did. Newspapers printed what the Communist Party told them to print. Traditional ink painting and literature gave way to new books, films, TV, art, and music that represented the ideals of the Cultural Revolution. Modern operas, orchestral symphonies, and ballets became "model works" for the people. Speech was censored: People overheard speaking critically of the government or its policies might soon find themselves in prison. Information from the outside was heavily censored, and most Chinese people had no idea what was happening in the world beyond their own country.

▶ The statement suggests that "sinister" trends in the arts were at the center of resistance to Mao and the revolution. This was part of an official statement made by the Communist Party forum on art and literature in Shanghai in February 1966. Many artists and writers subsequently became victims of the violence of the Cultural Revolution.

▼ Dancers perform during a 1967 production of the ballet, *Grassland Militia*. The approved artistic style was known as Socialist Realism. It combined realistic pictures or descriptions with an optimistic, pro-Communist view of life and events.

1

China is under the dictatorship of a sinister anti-Party and an anti-Socialist line which is diametrically opposed to Chairman Mao's thought. This sinister line is a combination of *bourgeois* (middle class) ideas on literature and art, modern revisionist ideas on literature and art, and . . . the [Nationalist] literature and art of the 1930s.

Communist Party statement, 1966

2

3

In the last seventeen years [since the foundation of the People's Republic of China] there have been some good or fairly good works in literature and art reflecting the workers, peasants, and soldiers. But most things were Famous, Foreign, or Fabled... in education we produced even more intellectuals than before who were completely cut off from the people. ... You can't have peaceful co-existence in this area of ideology [theory and ideas]. You co-exist and they'll corrupt you.

Jiang Qing, 1967

◀ In April 1967, Mao's third wife, Jiang Qing (1914-1991), praises Socialist Realism and attacks art she labels counter-revolutionary. Jiang claimed that most literature and art glorified old traditions or foreign ways of doing things. She understood that art influenced how people thought, and she allowed no art beyond the Socialist Realist movement. Many Chinese dramas and operas were rewritten to present the ideals of the Cultural Revolution.

4

▶ Jiang Qing at the height of her power in 1973, when she was known as the "Great Flag-carrier of the *Proletarian* (working class) Culture." Jiang controlled the arts and played a leading political role in China during the late 1960's and early 1970's. After Mao's death in 1976, the extremist group she formed—the *Gang of Four*—was discredited. Jiang was sentenced to life imprisonment for crimes committed during the Cultural Revolution. She committed suicide in 1991.

NOW YOU KNOW

- Nearly every aspect of life was subject to censorship in the People's Republic of China.
- Socialist Realism became the only approved art movement during the Cultural Revolution.
- Mao's wife, Jiang Qing, played a large role in the censorship of the arts.

Religion

CHINA'S COMMUNIST GOVERNMENT SAW RELIGION AS A THREAT TO ITS POWER. Karl Marx, whose writings formed the foundation of Communism, had condemned religion, and religious values represented a threatening alternative to Communist teachings. The Chinese Communists forbade most religious practices and destroyed many Taoist and Buddhist temples and other religious buildings. Many foreign missionaries and clergy were imprisoned or forced to leave China. Attacks on religion became even fiercer during the Cultural Revolution. Worship was restricted to Mao himself, with the Little Red Book as China's Bible. After Mao's death in 1976, the Chinese government allowed limited religious freedom.

1

". . . Why are so many Christian leaders still in prison? . . ." I asked him. "To my certain knowledge, there are four Roman Catholic bishops and three Protestants. . . . If that is not religious persecution, then what is it?"

Mr. Ho was distinctly uneasy . . . but he stuck manfully to his line.

"Oh, no!" he said. "None of these cases means religious persecution. In each case, the man concerned committed a political offence, even though he may have used the church, the pulpit, to hide what he was doing."

interview with Ho Chen-hsiang, 1956

◀ An Australian journalist interviews Ho Chen-hsiang, director of China's Bureau of Religious Affairs, in 1956. The Chinese government denied that it persecuted religion. Ho claimed that people were not locked up for their beliefs, but for political crimes against the government. But in China, a political crime could be anything. Religious teachings went against Communist ideas.

▶ The writer Jung Chang describes in her autobiography, *Wild Swans*, how young people were taught to view the Christian Church as something strange and sinister. Christianity seemed a foreign and frightening religion to many Chinese people. Churches with foreign headquarters, such as the Roman Catholic Church, were not allowed to operate in China.

2

The church was still functioning, under the control of the government, which had forced Catholics to break with the Vatican [the Roman Catholic Church] and join a "patriotic" organization. The idea of a Church was both mysterious and frightening, because of the propaganda about religion. . . . Priests also invariably appeared as imperialist spies [agents of foreign aggression] and evil people who used babies from orphanages for medical experiments.

Jung Chang, 1991

3 Demons taunt Buddha in the elaborate chapel of "The Temptation of Buddha." The chapel was in the 1,000-year-old Kyangphu Monastery in Tibet. Kyangphu and many other Buddhist monasteries, works of art, and sacred objects were destroyed during the Cultural Revolution.

NOW YOU KNOW

- The Communists saw religion as a threat to their power.
- The Communists destroyed churches and temples throughout China.
- Young people were taught to fear religion, especially Christianity.

Women and Family

I N TRADITIONAL CHINESE SOCIETY, WOMEN WERE SEEN AS INFERIOR TO MEN. Women had to obey their fathers and husbands, and families valued sons more than daughters. A husband could divorce his wife if she failed to give birth to sons. In some cases, daughters were killed at birth to save resources. Parents arranged marriages for their children, choosing whom the children would marry. The Communist government stressed that families should value girls and boys equally. They banned arranged marriages and supported the idea that women should contribute to the family income and participate in social and political activities. Some women began to work outside the home, but the vast majority remained in traditional roles.

◀ Female machinists inspect their equipment at a Beijing tool plant in 1956. In Communist China, women developed new skills and became involved in new occupations. Many women carried out the harsh manual labor involved in China's ambitious construction projects.

▶ A 1958 party statement stresses the Communist belief that communal society would largely replace the traditional family. Tasks and responsibilities—including the raising of children—were shared between all members of the communes. This was meant to break the traditional bonds of family and remove differences between men and women.

The framework of the individual family, which has existed for thousands of years, has been shattered for all time. . . . We must regard the People's Commune as our family and not pay too much attention to forming a separate family of our own.

Communist Party statement, 1958

3

◀ A woman displays the results of foot binding, a traditional Chinese practice. The feet of upper and middle class girls were tightly bound so that, as they grew, the feet became bent over and deformed but appeared to be very small. This was considered to be elegant, though it was painful and prevented women from walking properly. Foot binding also helped to keep women dependent on their male relatives. China's Communist government banned the practice.

4

> In order to build a great socialist society it is of the utmost importance to arouse the broad masses of women to join in productive activity. Men and women must receive equal pay for equal work in production. Genuine equality between the sexes can only be realized in the process of the socialist transformation of society as a whole.
>
> China's women are a vast reserve of labour power. This reserve should be tapped in the struggle to build a great socialist country.
>
> Mao Zedong, 1955

▶ In introductions he wrote to a 1955 government publication, Mao seems to see women in a contradictory light: On the one hand, they should gain full equality; on the other, they offer a vast source of untapped labor.

NOW YOU KNOW

- In traditional Chinese society, women were treated as inferiors.
- The Communist government banned arranged marriage and foot binding.
- The Communists encouraged women to work and socialize outside the home.

Population, Health, and Education

CHINA'S POPULATION GREW STEADILY UNDER COMMUNIST RULE. The Chinese government faced huge problems taking care of its many people. In 1949, the vast majority of Chinese were illiterate. Most people had never seen a doctor, and there was never enough food for everyone. After the revolution, schools were built and teachers trained. New hospitals housed new doctors and nurses. A corps of peasant doctors—the "barefoot doctors"—brought medicine to rural areas for the first time. But food production declined, and millions of people starved to death. The Cultural Revolution then reversed most of the government's small advances. Schools and universities were shut down. Educated people were regarded with mistrust, and many professors, scientists, doctors, and artists were imprisoned, killed, or driven from the country.

1

▶ Mao praises population growth in 1949, during the early days of the regime. Mao regarded China's huge population as a source of strength and believed the country's manpower could make up for its lack of advanced skills and modern technology. Food production did not keep up with population growth, however. Tens of millions of Chinese people starved to death during Mao's reign.

A large population in China is a very good thing. With a population increase of several fold we still have an adequate solution. The solution lies in production. The fallacy [mistaken belief] of the Western capitalist economists ... that the increase in food lags behind the increase of population was long ago refuted [proved wrong].
Mao Zedong, 1949

2

Intellectuals are teachers employed by the working class and the laboring people to teach their children. If they go against the wishes of their masters and insist on teaching their own set of subjects, teaching stereotyped writing, Confucian classics, or capitalist rubbish, and turn out a number of counter-revolutionaries, the working class will not tolerate it and will sack them and not renew their contract for the coming year.
Mao Zedong, 1957

◀ Mao expresses his view of education in July 1957 speech. He believed the education system should teach Communist Party values only. As servants of the workers and peasants, teachers who disobeyed the Party were betraying the people. Offending teachers were fired, beaten, or imprisoned.

3

▲ A "barefoot doctor" treats a patient in rural China before the Cultural Revolution. "Barefoot doctors" were trained in basic medicine to examine and treat peasants throughout China's vast countryside. They gave first aid, immunizations, taught hygiene, and organized sanitation campaigns. Medical cases beyond their training were referred to regular doctors at local commune centers. The program provided millions of peasants with health care for the first time in their lives.

NOW YOU KNOW

- China's rising population presented difficult problems for the Communist government.
- Attempts were made to increase educational opportunities and improve medical care.
- The Cultural Revolution disrupted China's progress in health care and education.

China—A Nuclear Power

CHINA FOUND FEW ALLIES IN THE 1950'S AND 1960'S. Even fellow Communist nations like the Soviet Union—originally China's most important ally—distanced themselves from the radical leaders of China. China found itself sandwiched between the intimidating nuclear threats of both the Soviet Union and the United States. China refused to participate in a 1963 partial nuclear test ban agreement with the Soviets and the West. The following year, in October 1964, China successfully tested its first atomic bomb.

◀ Chinese Premier Zhou Enlai (far left) welcomes Indian Prime Minister Jawaharlal Nehru (1889-1964) and his daughter, Indira Gandhi (1917-1984), to Beijing in October 1954. China tried to befriend India, but relations soured after the Tibetan uprising in 1959. Increasing tensions led to a brief border war between China and India in 1962.

▶ In a 1955 speech, Zhou Enlai seeks the cooperation of African and Asian at an international conference in Bandung, Indonesia. Zhou, China's foreign minister from 1949 to 1958, asked the countries to disregard their differences and unite in the struggle against domination by Western powers like the United Kingdom and United States.

The Chinese delegation [group at the conference] has come for the purpose of seeking unity, not to pick quarrels. There is no need to trumpet one's ideology [political ideas], or the differences that exist among us. We are here to seek a community of views, not to raise points of difference. . . . Most of the countries of Asia and Africa have suffered from colonialism [political domination by another country]. . . . We are economically backward. . . . If we seek common ground to remove the misery imposed upon us, it will be easy for us to understand each other, to respect each other, to help each other.

Premier Zhou Enlai, 1955

3

▶ The Chinese government responds to the signing of the 1963 Partial Test Ban Treaty by the Soviet Union, United Kingdom, and United States. The treaty was meant to slow the arms race and limit the release of nuclear radiation into Earth's atmosphere. The Chinese saw it as a plot by the three powers to prevent other countries from developing their own weapons.

The central purpose of this treaty is, through a partial ban on nuclear tests, to prevent all the threatened peace-loving countries, including China, from increasing their defense capability, so that the United States may be more unbridled in threatening and blackmailing these countries.

Chinese government statement, 1963

4

◀ China detonates its first nuclear weapon on Oct. 16, 1964, in the deserts of Xinjiang in far northwestern China. The Chinese government proudly announced the successful test to the world, calling it a "major achievement" against Western threats and oppression. With nuclear weapons and the world's largest standing army —in excess of 1 million troops—China had become a powerful military force.

NOW YOU KNOW

- Few countries allied with China in the 1950's and 1960's.
- China felt threatened by the partial nuclear test ban treaty of 1963.
- China successfully tested its first nuclear weapon in October 1964.

China Joins the United Nations

THE PEOPLE'S REPUBLIC OF CHINA TOOK CONTROL OF MAINLAND CHINA IN 1949, but China's seat at the United Nations (UN) continued to be held by Chiang Kai-shek's Republic of China on Taiwan. Several attempts to change the situation were blocked, mainly by the United States. However, support for the Communist government in Beijing grew over time, especially after its development of nuclear weapons. The admission of several newly independent African nations into the UN in the 1960's finally gave mainland China enough votes to gain entry, and in 1971, it replaced Taiwan in the United Nations. Although it has tried several times, the Taiwan has never regained a seat in the UN.

1

. . . to restore all its rights to the People's Republic of China and to recognize the representatives of its Government as the only legitimate representatives of China to the United Nations, and to expel *forthwith* [immediately] the representatives of Chiang Kai-shek from the place which they unlawfully occupy at the United Nations and in all the organizations related to it.

UN Resolution 2758
Oct. 25, 1971

◄ The United Nations announces its support for the People's Republic of China in 1971 in Resolution 2758. The resolution expelled Chiang Kai-shek's Nationalists, who had held the Chinese seat at the United Nations since its foundation in 1945. The resolution was passed with 76 votes in favor, 35 against, and 17 not voting.

2

► Tanzanian President Julius Nyerere (1922-1999) thanks China for a loan to begin construction on the Tazara Railway in 1970. The railway connected Tanzania with its neighbor Zambia. Without the Chinese loan, the two African nations could not have afforded to build the $500 million railway. Such gestures earned support for China's membership in the UN. Tazara stands for Tanzania-Zambia Railway Authority.

We are extremely grateful to the Chinese People's Republic. . . . Let me state quite clearly that we appreciate this loan, and we appreciate the fact that it is interest-free. We greatly appreciate all this help with the building of our railway. And—I repeat— the Chinese people have not asked us to become Communists in order to qualify for this loan!
Julius Nyerere, 1970

▲ Representatives of the Republic of China on Taiwan leave the United Nations General Assembly on Oct. 25, 1971. After 22 years of existence, the People's Republic of China had been recognized as the lawful government of China by the United Nations.

NOW YOU KNOW

- Chiang Kai-shek's Nationalist government gained the Chinese seat in the UN in 1945.
- Support from new African nations aided the PRC's campaign to join the UN.
- The People's Republic of China displaced Taiwan in the UN in 1971.

U.S. President Nixon Visits China

THE PEOPLE'S REPUBLIC OF CHINA (PRC) AND THE UNITED STATES did not establish diplomatic relations at the time of the PRC's founding in 1949. To correct this, U.S. foreign affairs advisor Henry Kissinger (1923-) made a secret trip to Beijing in 1971. During this trip, Kissinger made a series of deals with the Chinese, paving the way for peaceful relations. In February 1972, U.S. President Richard Nixon (1913-1994) shocked the world by traveling to China to meet with Chairman Mao Zedong and Premier Zhou Enlai. The leaders agreed to solve their problems peacefully while joining in opposition to the Soviet Union. The Americans would continue to protect Taiwan, but recognize it as part of China, while also discouraging any renewed Japanese expansion.

▲ Zhou Enlai and Richard Nixon inspect Chinese troops in Beijing on Feb. 26, 1972. During Nixon's historic trip, he met with Mao and visited the Great Wall and the cities of Hangzhou and Shanghai.

2

Most memorable were my meetings with Chou [Zhou Enlai] and Mao. We learned later that Mao had already suffered a mild stroke, although the Chinese people did not know it. He was still treated with enormous respect by his aides and attendants and was sharp in his *repartee* [conversation]. . . . His office was cluttered with books—not for show, but for reading . . . he said he had read *Six Crises* [by Nixon] and found that "it was not a bad book". . . . He showed his political *acumen* [shrewdness] when he said, "I voted for you during your last election."

Richard Nixon, 1990

◀ In Nixon's memoir, *In the Arena*, the former president recalls his surprisingly friendly meeting with Mao Zedong. Nixon was impressed with Mao's intelligence and the loyalty he inspired in those around him. Nixon's visit to China began the process leading to formal recognition of China by the United States in 1979.

▶ In his autobiography, *The White House Years*, Henry Kissinger explains the importance of Nixon's visit to China. The Shanghai Communiqué was a joint statement issued by the United States and China. It was the first step in creating normal relations between the two countries.

3

The Shanghai Communiqué . . . served to highlight the revolutionary change in the Chinese–American relationship. . . . China and the United States in effect renounced the use of force in settling disputes with each other. They announced their common opposition to the *hegemonic aspirations* [political domination] of others. They agreed not to enter into any agreements aimed at the other. They undertook to promote exchanges and trade. And Taiwan was handled in a manner preserving the dignity, self-respect, and commitments of each side.

Henry Kissinger, 1979

NOW YOU KNOW

- Until 1972, the People's Republic of China and the United States had no official diplomatic relations.
- Henry Kissinger's secret trip to China paved the way for Nixon's visit in 1972.
- The Shanghai Communiqué expressed a desire for peaceful relations and marked the beginning of proper contacts between China and the United States.

End of the Revolution?

MAO ZEDONG DIED IN 1976 AND DENG XIAOPING BECAME CHINA'S PRIMARY LEADER. Deng had been disgraced during the Cultural Revolution, but he survived and returned to power. Deng's government publicly denounced Mao's radical supporters, including his wife, Jiang Qing. Jiang and three of her followers—"the Gang of Four"—were removed from their positions and arrested. Deng opened China to the outside world and allowed individuals and companies to operate for profits, that is, to make money. Deng used ideas from both Communism and other systems of government to modernize China. By the time of his death in 1997, little remained of Mao's revolution-driven society.

1

Communist society will not flourish in a courtyard behind locked doors. Opening the country to the outside world is . . . not an *expedient measure* [a short-term solution] but a fundamental principle for building a socialist society, as well as the only road to a communist society.

Li Honglin, 1984

◀ In an October 1984 *People's Daily* newspaper essay, theorist Li Honglin explains China's need to interact with the outside world. Li believed that socialist and Communist tradition depended upon an open society.

▼ In 2000, a cyclist rides past a billboard on which pictures of earlier Chinese leaders Deng Xiaoping (left) and Mao Zedong (center) are shown alongside then Communist Party chief, Jiang Zemin (1926-). Although later leaders changed many of Mao's policies and acknowledged some of his mistakes, Mao is still celebrated as a hero by the Chinese government.

2

3

▶ In a 1986 interview with Mike Wallace on the television show *60 Minutes*, Deng explains his view of wealth quite different from Mao Zedong's. To Mao, allowing some people to become rich could only lead to a capitalist class that would undermine Communism and dominate the rest of the people. China's economy grew and living conditions improved under Deng. However, the changes led to inflation and created greater social inequality.

The main task in the socialist stage is to develop the productive forces, keep increasing the material wealth of society, steadily improve the life of the people and create material conditions for the advent of a communist society. There can be no communism with pauperism [extreme poverty], or socialism with pauperism. So to get rich is no sin.

Deng Xiaoping, 1986

4

◀ Investors watch a stock exchange board in Shanghai on March 23, 2009. Stock exchanges are places where shares in companies are bought and sold. In Communist countries, companies are generally state owned, so there are no stock exchanges. But in 1990, the first modern Chinese exchange was opened, taking the People's Republic of China further from its Communist roots.

NOW YOU KNOW

- After Mao's death in 1976, Deng Xiaoping emerged as China's top leader.
- Jiang Qing and her radical followers were removed from power and arrested.
- Deng opened China to the outside world and improved its economy and standard of living.

Timeline

1911	A revolution against imperial rule breaks out in China.
Feb. 12, 1912	The last emperor abdicates and China becomes a republic.
1916	The republican government weakens and much of China is ruled by local warlords.
May 4, 1919	Demonstrations in Beijing against the plan to hand over German holdings in China to the Japanese.
1921	The Chinese Communist Party is founded in Shanghai.
June 1923	Under pressure from Soviet advisors, the Chinese Communist Party forms an alliance with the Nationalists against the warlords.
March 12, 1925	Sun Yat-sen dies; Chiang Kai-shek replaces him as leader of the Nationalist Party.
April 12, 1927	The Nationalists turn on their Communist allies and massacre thousands of them. Civil war breaks out between the Nationalists and Communists.
Sept. 19, 1931	The Japanese invade the northeastern Chinese province of Manchuria.
1934–1935	The Nationalists drive the Chinese Communist Party from its bases in southern China and the Communists retreat 6,000 miles on their famous "Long March." Mao emerges as the Communist leader.
Dec. 12, 1936	Chiang Kai-shek is kidnapped and forced to ally with the Communists against the Japanese.
July 7, 1937	Japan begins a full-scale invasion of China.
Dec. 8, 1941	World War II reaches the Far East when the United States declares war on Japan following the attack on Pearl Harbor.
August 15, 1945	Japan surrenders.
1946–1949	Civil war breaks out again between the Communists and Nationalists. The Communists win and the Nationalists flee to Taiwan.
Oct. 1, 1949	Mao Zedong proclaims the People's Republic of China.
June 25, 1950	Communist North Korea invades South Korea. A UN coalition led by the United States intervenes to defend the South.
October	Chinese armies move into Tibet.
October	U.S. forces approach the Chinese border. China joins the war, siding with North Korea.
July 27, 1953	The Korean war ends in a stalemate.
June, 1957	Mao launches the short-lived Hundred Flowers movement, encouraging criticism of the Communist Party.
1958	A five-year plan, the Great Leap Forward, aims to industrialize China rapidly and reorganize farmers into huge agricultural communes. Its failure causes a terrible famine.
March 1959	Tibetans rise in protest against Chinese Communist rule, but are defeated by the Red Army. The Dalai Lama flees to India.
1961	The Soviet–Chinese alliance ends.
Oct. 16, 1964	China carries out its first successful nuclear test.
July 1966	Mao signals his return to the center of Chinese politics.
August–November	Mao launches the Cultural Revolution. Mao and Lin Biao hold rallies to encourage young people to become Red Guards.
February 1967	With China in chaos, the army moves to control the Red Guards.
Sept. 13, 1971	After a failed attempt at a coup, Lin Biao dies in a plane crash.
Oct. 25	The Republic of China on Taiwan is expelled from the UN and the People's Republic takes its place.
February 1972	Richard Nixon becomes the first U.S. president to visit Communist China.
Sept. 9, 1976	Mao Zedong dies.
1978	Deng Xiaoping emerges as China's leader and begins to reverse many of Mao's policies.

Sources

4–5 Document 2– Fu, Zengxiang. 1919. In Schwarcz, Vera. *The Chinese Enlightenment.* University of California Press, 1986. Print. Document 3 – Sun, Yat-sen. Speech. Jan. 1924. In Mackerras, Colin. *China in Transformation 1900-1949.* New York: Longman, 1998. Print.

6–7 Document 1 – Mao, Zedong. "On Tactics Against Japanese Imperialism." 27 Dec. 1935. In *Selected works of Mao Tse-tung.* Vol. 1. Foreign Language Press, 1965. Print. Document 4 – Deng, Xiaoping. *Red Star* [newspaper] editorial. 11 Nov. 1934. In Sun, Shuyun.*The Long March.* New York: Double Day, 2006. Print.

8–9 Document 1 – Mao, Zedong. 1934. In Sun, Shuyun.*The Long March.* New York: Double Day, 2006. Print. Document 3 – Rabe, John. *The Good Man of Nanking.* New York: Knopf, 1998. Print.

10–11 Document 1 – Zhu, De. Interview. 1937. In Bertram, James. *Unconquered.* New York: John Day, 1939. Print. Document 2 – Vladimirov, Peter. 1942. In Vladimirov, Peter P. *The Vladimirov Diaries.* Garden City, NY: Doubleday, 1975. Print. Document 3 – Stillwell, Joseph W. *The Stillwell Papers.* 1948. New York: Da Capo, 1991. Print.

12–13 Document 1 – Mao, Zedong. Reissue of the Three Main Rules of Discipline and the Eight Points for Attention. 10 Oct. 1947. In *Selected Works of Mao Tse-tung.* Vol. 4. Foreign Language Press, 1961. Print. Document 2 – Marshall, George C. 1947. In Lawrance, Alan. *China since 1919.* New York: Routledge, 2004. Print.

14–15 Document 1 – Mao, Zedong. Speech. 21 Sept. 1949. In *Selected Works of Mao Tse-tung.* Vol. 5. Foreign Language Press, 1977. Print. Document 3 – Hu, Feng. "Song of Joy." 1949. *Twentieth Century Chinese Poetry.* Garden City, NY: Doubleday, 1963. Print.

16–17 Document 1 – Mao, Zedong. *Some Questions Concerning Methods of Leadership.* 1 June 1943. In *Selected Works of Mao Tse-tung.* Vol. 3. Foreign Language Press, 1965. Print. Document 3 – Bodde, Derk. *Peking Diary.* New York: Octagon Books, 1976. Print.

18–19 Document 1 – *Hsin Hwa Pao* [newspaper] editorial. 2 Sept. 1949. In Tsering Shakya. *The Dragon in the Land of Snows.* Columbia University Press, 1999. Print. Document 3 – Sinha, S. Report to the government of India. 16 Apr. 1952. In Tsering Shakya. *The Dragon in the Land of Snows.* Columbia University Press, 1999. Print.

20–21 Document 1 – Kuo, Cheng k'uan. In Hinton, William. *Fanshen.* University of California Press, 1966. Print. Document 3 – Mao, Anying. 1950. In Chang, Jung, and Jon Halliday. *Mao: The Unknown Story.* New York: Knopf, 2005. Print.

22–23 Document 1 – Mao, Zedong. "Order to the Chinese People's Volunteers." 8 Oct. 1950. In *Selected Works of Mao Tse-tung.* Vol. 5. Foreign Language Press, 1977. Print. Document 3 – Allen, Norman. Letter to his mother. 4 Nov. 1950. In *The Cold War: A History in Documents and Eyewitness Accounts.* New York: Oxford, 2004. Print.

24–25 Document 1 – Wu, Kuo-chen. Open letter to the National Assembly. 27 Feb. 1954. In Kerr, George H. *Formosa Betrayed.* Boston: Houghton Mifflin, 1965. Print. Document 3 – "Formosa: Man of the Single Truth." *Time* 18 Apr. 1955: 32+. Print.

26–27 Document 1 – Dai, Huang. *Jiusi yisheng* [Narrow Escape from Death], 1998. In Chang, Jung, and Jon Halliday. *Mao: The Unknown Story.* New York: Knopf, 2005. Print. Document 2 – Lin, His-ling. Speech at Peking University. 1957. In Doolin, Dennis J. *Communist China: The Politics of Student Opposition.* Hoover Institution, 1964. Print.

28–29 Document 1 – Chinese man's interview with an historian. 1995. In Sang, Ye. "1959 & its Aftermath." *China Heritage Quarterly.* Web. 20 May 2010. Document 3 – Liu, Shaoqi. Report delivered at the Eighth CCP National Congress. 5 May 1958. In *A Documentary History of Communism.* Vol. 2. London: Tauris, 1986. Print.

30–31 Document 2 – Peng, Dehuai. Letter to Mao Zedong. 1959. In Benson, Linda. *China since 1949.* Harlow: Longman, 2002. Print. Document 3 – Wei, Wu-ji. Famine account. 1961. In *Social Suffering.* University of California Press, 1997. Print.

32–33 Document 1 – Hsi Chang-hao, and Kao Yuan-mei. *Tibet Leaps Forward.* Foreign Language Press, 1977. Print. Document 3 – The Panchen Lama. May 1962. In Tsering Shakya. "Blood in the Snows." *New Left Review* 15 (2002): Web. 26 May 2010.

34–35 Document 1 – Liu, Shaoqi. Report to a Communist conference. Jan. 1962. In Dittmer, Lowell. *Liu Shaoqi and the Chinese Cultural Revolution.* Armonk, N.Y.: M.E. Sharpe, 1998. Print. Document 3 – Deng, Xiaoping. Speech to the Communist Youth League. 7 July 1962. In *Selected Works of Deng Xiaoping, 1938-1965.* Foreign Language Press, 1992. Print.

36–37 Document 2 – Editors of People's Daily and Red Flag. *On Khrushchov's Phony Communism...* Foreign Language Press, 1964. Print. Document 3 – Chen, Yi. Interview with the editor of a Uruguay newspaper. 1966. InTsou, Tang. *The Cultural Revolution and Post-Mao Reforms.* University of Chicago Press, 1986. Print.

38–39 Document 1 – Lin, Biao. Foreword of *Quotations from Chairman Mao Tse-tung.* Foreign Language Press, 1967. Print. Document 3 – Liu, Tao. 1966. In Dittmer, Lowell. *Liu Shaoqi and the Chinese Cultural Revolution.* Armonk, N.Y.: M.E. Sharpe, 1998. Print.

40–41 Document 1 – Xie, Fuzhi. Speech. 1966. In Short, Philip. *Mao: A Life.* New York: Holt, 2001. Print. Document 3 – Chang, Jung. *Wild Swans.* New York: Simon & Schuster, 1991. Print.

42–43 Document 1 – Gao, Xingjian. *One Man's Bible.* New York: HarperCollins, 2002. Print. Document 3 – "The East is Red." In Sun, Shuyun. *The Long March.* New York: Doubleday, 2006. Print.

44–45 Document 1 – Communist Party statement on art and literature. 1966. In He. Henry Yuhuai. *Dictionary of the Political Thought of the People's Republic of China.* Armonk, N.Y.: M.E. Sharpe, 2001. Print. Document 3 – Jiang, Qing. Speech. 1967. In Gittings, John. *The Changing Face of China.* New York: Oxford, 2006. Print.

46–47 Document 1 – Ho, Chen-hsiang. Interview. 1956. In MacInnis, Donald E., comp. *Religious Policy and Practice in Communist China.* New York: MacMillan, 1972. Print. Document 2 – Chang, Jung. *Wild Swans.* New York: Simon & Schuster, 1991. Print.

48–49 Document 2 – Chinese Communist Party statement. 1958. In Becker, Jasper. *Hungry Ghosts.* New York: Henry Holt, 1996. Print. Document 4 – Mao, Zedong. Introductory notes to "Women Have Gone to the Labour Front" and "Solving the Labour Shortage by Arousing the Women to Join in Production" *The Socialist Upsurge in China's Countryside,* Vols. I & II, 1955. Print.

50–51 Document 1 – Mao, Zedong. 1949. In Coale, Ansley J. *Proceedings of the National Academy of Sciences of the United States of America* 80.6 (1983): 1757–1763. Print. Document 2 – Zedong, Mao. Speech. 9 July 1957. In *Selected works of Mao Tse-tung.* Vol. 5. Foreign Language Press, 1977. Print.

52–53 Document 2 – Zhou, Enlai. Speech at the Bandung Conference. Apr. 1955. In Han, Suyin. *Eldest Son.* New York: Kondansha, 1995. Print. Document 3 – Chinese government statement on the Partial Test Ban Treaty. 31 July 1963. In Lawrance, Alan. *China's Foreign Relations Since 1949.* London: Routledge, 1975. Print.

54–55 Document 1 – United Nations General Assembly. Resolution 2758 (XXVI). 25 Oct. 1971. *United Nations.* Web. 27 May 2010. Document 2 – Nyerere, Julius K. Speech. 28 Oct. 1970. In *Freedom and Development.* New York: Oxford, 1973. Print.

56–57 Document 2 – Nixon, Richard M. *In the Arena.* New York: Simon & Schuster, 1990. Print. Document 3 – Kissinger, Henry. *The White House Years.* London : Weidenfeld and Nicolson, 1979. Print.

58–59 Document 1 – Li, Honglin. Essay in *The Peoples Daily* [Chinese newspaper]. 15 Oct. 1984. In Gittings, John. *The Changing Face of China.* New York: Oxford, 2005. Print. Document 3 – Deng, Xiaoping. Interview by Mike Wallace. *60 Minutes.* CBS. 2 Sept. 1986.

Additional Resources

Books

The Aftermath of the Chinese Nationalist Revolution, by Kathlyn Gay, Twenty-First Century Books, 2008

China's Son: Growing Up in the Cultural Revolution, by Da Chen, Laurel Leaf, 2004

The Oriole's Song: An American Girlhood in Wartime China, by Betty Jean Rugh, Eastbridge, 2003

Red Scarf Girl: A Memoir of the Cultural Revolution, by Ji-Li Jiang, HarperCollins, 2008

Websites

http://archives.cbc.ca/politics/international_politics/topics/2049/
The Canadian Broadcasting Company (CBC) created this interactive site on "Revolution and Evolution in Modern China."

http://hoover.archives.gov/exhibits/China/Political%20Evolution/index.html
The Herbert Hoover Presidential Library and Museum created this fascinating collection on "The Political Evolution of China."

http://news.bbc.co.uk/hi/english/static/special_report/1999/09/99/china_50/nodhtml.htm
The British Broadcasting Company (BBC) created this comprehensive interactive special report on "China's Communist Revolution."

http://topics.nytimes.com/topics/reference/timestopics/people/m/mao_zedong/index.html
The *New York Times* compiled this list of articles and resources on Mao Zedong.

Index

Acknowledgements

AKG-Images: 6, 9, (North Wind Picture Archives), 8; **American-Rails.com:** 21 (Resource guide to American railroading); **Art Archives:** 22 (Domenica del Corriere/Gianni Dagli Orti); **Bridgeman Art Library: AKG-Images:** 27, (Ullstein Bild), 29, 44 (Zhou Thong); **BH © Link:** 30, 31, 51; **Bridgeman Art Library:** 14, 28, 38, 40, 42 (© The Chambers Galley, London), 39 (© Private Collection); **Corbis:** 8, 22, 56, 9, 11, 13, 18, 33, 48, 53, (© Bettmann), 34 (© Arthur Rothstein), 36 (© The Dmitri Baltermants Collection), 23 (© Hulton-Deutsch Collection), 43 (© Owen Franken), 55 (© Sygma), 49 (© Underwood & Underwood), 17 (© Yves Gellie); **CSU Archives:** 20 (Everett Collection/Rex Features); **Getty:** 4, 59, 19, 32, 35, 45, 52, 58 (AFP); **Rex Features:** 6, 7, (Pacific Press), 5, 21 (Roger-Violett), 15, (Sipa Press 255550), **Topfoto:** 41, (Ullstein Bild), 47 (Alinari), 16, (AP), 30, 31, 25, (The Image Works), 25, 35, (Topham Picturepoint). **U.S. Navy:** 24.

Cover main image: **Lonely Planet Images;** inset image: **Corbis**